CW00521809

Pet Rats
for Beginners

Species Appropriate Care for the Clever Fluffbutts

ALINA DARIA

ISBN: 9798521708796

Contents

Introduction

The scientific name of the rat genus is "Rattus". These animals belong to the rodents and are classified as mice-like (Muroidea). Furthermore, the rat genus belongs to the long-tailed mouse family (Muridae).

But not all rats are the same - within this genus, about 65 different species are known. These are mostly to be found in Asia and Australia; on the other continents, rather fewer rat species exist. The most widespread rat species are the *roof rat (or: black rat)* and the *Norway rat.*

The scientific name of roof rats is "Rattus rattus". The scientific name of Norway rats is "Rattus norvegicus".

As a rule, however, the so-called fancy rats are kept as pets. These are descended from the Norway rat - the Norway rat is therefore the wild form, and the fancy rat is the domesticated form of this species. The domesticated fancy rat was created by deliberate breeding in order to keep rats as pets.

At the beginning of the twentieth century, people found pleasure in the rat as a pet. But even before that, rat catchers, for example, began to study the animals in detail. This probably began in the nineteenth century at the latest. Initially, the aim of these rat catchers was to study the animals and analyse their behaviour in order to be able to catch the wild animals more easily.

A famous British rat catcher was called Jack Black and probably lived between 1800 and 1850. Among other things, he worked as a rat catcher or exterminator for the then Queen Victoria. Jack Black began quite early to tame Norway rats and then sell them to people who were interested in rats as pets. Over time, the animals became tamer and tamer as they became domesticated.

Unfortunately, rats were then also bred as laboratory animals. The Norway / fancy rats were and are used in laboratories and for animal testing.

© *Sibya*

Through years of breeding, many different colourings of rats developed. Therefore, domesticated breeding forms are often quite easy to distinguish from the wild forms.

The name "fancy rat" became established for this domesticated form of rat - however, they are also often referred to as "laboratory rats" due to their use in research laboratories. The scientific name for domesticated rats is "*Rattus norvegicus domestica*".

Domesticated fancy rats can be distinguished from Norway rats not only by colouration, but also by changes in body structure and body functions. However, the differences between fancy rats and Norway rats are not considered serious enough to justify a new, separate subspecies.

Pet rats are usually quite tame or at least can be tamed easily. They usually feel very comfortable with their owners and often seek the proximity of their human companions. Most pet rats have no problem with touching and often seek physical contact themselves.

In addition, domesticated pet rats are also less skittish than their wild comrades. This is probably because they have less to fear from danger. They are used to a largely safe life with safe food.

Most Norway rats - that is, rats in the wild - are dark brown. Random colour mutations can also occur in the wild, but this does not happen too often.

The colours of fancy rats, on the other hand, are often deliberately bred and are very diverse - they come in black, white, cinnamon, etc. In addition, pet rats can have piebald fur.

The anatomy of pet rats is also no longer identical to that of Norway rats. Pet rats usually have a smaller body, a longer tail and also larger ears.

The life expectancy of pet rats is approximately between two and four years. This means they have a longer life expectancy than wild Norway rats, which often only live for one year. However, this is not due to physiology, but rather to the fact that wild rats are exposed to greater dangers such as enemies and lack of food.

© *Firelong*

Colour and Fur

In many domesticated animals, a wide variety of colours and furs have been bred over many decades. This is not only the case with rats, but also with hamsters, guinea pigs, for example. While the wild Norway rat is in almost all cases plain brown and has the same fur structure, the bred pet rats can now be found in many varieties. Of course, some domesticated rats still have the original brown colouring of the wild Norway rats (agouti). In addition, there are, for example, black, white, beige and chocolate rats - and of course rats that can have multiple colours or a piebald pattern.

The same genes that are responsible for the colouring of the fur also determine the eye colour of the rat. The rat may have ruby, pinkish or black eyes. In some cases, a rat also has two different eye colours ("odd-eyed").

The colour markings can also be quite varied. A solid-coloured animal is called "self". An overall white animal with coloured fur on the snout and foot area is called "Himalayan". A rat with a white belly and coloured back is called a "Berkshire". A rat with spots on the fur is called - like the dog - "Dalmatian". And a rat with a stripe on the belly side, whose colour corresponds to the colouring on the back side, is called "Downunder". There are also other fur types. However, it should not go unmentioned that the colouring and the markings do not influence the character of the animal. They only differ in appearance. Rats, like many other animal species, have very individual character traits, but these are not related to colour.

The fur structure can also differ. The vast majority of rats have "normal" fur, like that of the wild Norway rat - this fur tends to be thick and coarse but can also be somewhat finer in females. There are also rats with curly fur ("rex"), particularly soft and shimmering fur ("satin") and a few others.

Hairless rats are also quite common nowadays; these include the double rex and patchwork varieties, but also general naked "sphynx" rats. Keeping hairless rats is not advisable. Rats depend on their fur.

If they do not have fur, rats - and other species that have had their fur bred away - are more susceptible to disease and they are much more sensitive. They are less tolerant of cold, injure themselves more often, suffer more frequently from skin diseases and even often from organ diseases such as liver or kidney failure.

In addition, there are breeds that alter physical features such as the ears or tail. A rat with very large round ears that are set low is called a *dumbo rat*. The ears do not sit on top of the head, but rather lower on the side of the head. Dumbo rats are often referred to as torture breed. Torment breeds are breeding forms through which the animals suffer physical damage and disadvantages - i.e., when the breeding form leads to underperformance and/or when the animals suffer pain.

However, whether dumbo rats are actually a torture breed is highly controversial. At this stage, at least, there is no evidence that the animals suffer or are otherwise affected by the altered ears. However, deformations of the skeleton often occur in dumbo rats as well, which can be a sign that dumbos might be a torture breed.

The breeding form "Manx" (also called "Bobtail") is different. Manx rats are predominantly regarded as torture breeds because their tails have been bred away - they are tailless. That this is a type of torture breeding is mostly undisputed, as rats rely heavily on their tails.

They use the tail for thermoregulation. In addition, animal species that have a tail use it to balance themselves, for example, when climbing, and to keep their balance. This is not only the case with small animals like rats, but also with cats, for example. Furthermore, this type of breeding often shows deformities of the skeleton.

© Angelic Cooke

Group and Socialisation

Rats are extremely social animals and live in groups. Humans cannot replace companions of the same species and it is not in the nature of a rat to have only humans as friends.

A group should consist of at least three rats. Therefore, keeping rats alone or in pairs is not appropriate for the species and should be avoided. Rats interact with each other, are there for each other and sometimes quarrel. They groom each other, often eat together and sometimes play together. In addition, conspecifics provide a sense of security and community. All of this would be lost if a rat were kept individually.

Many rats that have to live in solitary confinement sooner or later display strange behavioural idiosyncrasies. One of these behavioural disorders is gnawing on the cage. Such behaviour can also be observed in other small animals that are bored and/or uncomfortable in solitary confinement. Due to the monotony of a solitary life, many rats also start to simply walk in circles or pluck out their fur. They get bored and feel lonely.

When rats live in solitary confinement, they often become very affectionate. They become extremely focused on the human, who is the centre of their life - and often the only meaning of their life. Inexperienced owners are often happy about this great expression of affection and assume that the rat is happy and loves its owner very much. And that is probably true. However, this behaviour is not healthy. It is wonderful when rats have a good relationship with their owners, do not shy away from touching and also often seek closeness. However, this does not replace contact with conspecifics. Humans and rats communicate differently and interact differently with each other. How would we feel if we only had rats for company and never saw another human being?

© *Varga*

Even other animal species cannot replace contact with conspecifics. Rats might get along well with other species, but they cannot communicate with each other and show different behaviour. Sometimes it can even lead to fatal fights. Since rats belong to the mice family, one might think that rats certainly get along well with mice. However, this is not the case and socialisation should be avoided in any case.

Rats and mice are not considered friends in the wild and mice are often injured by rats as they may be considered prey. Of course, this is not always the case; nevertheless, this risk should not be taken in order to protect the animals.

Socialising with other small animals such as guinea pigs, hamsters, rabbits, etc. is therefore also not recommended. On the one hand, these animal species have completely different needs and lifestyles than rats. On the other hand, such a combination can also lead to serious injuries.

So, a rat group should therefore consist of at least three rats. The animals should be of the same gender - so ideally you keep at least three girls together or at least three boys. In mixed groups (exception: see below), offspring can be expected regularly, even if the rats are related - because rats do not distinguish whether they reproduce with a relative (parents, children, siblings) or with a non-family rat.

This would mean incest and/or uncontrolled regular offspring. There are important factors to consider when breeding animals - genetics, for example. If mated incorrectly, significant health problems can arise. Therefore, breeding should be left to very experienced and reputable breeders.

Another possibility is harem keeping. In this case, a neutered (!) male lives together with several females. In order to fulfil the requirements of a pack, a neuter should live together with at least two females. After castration, reproduction is no longer possible.

Integrating new rats into an existing group can be quite difficult under certain circumstances. The rats in the group know each other and the daily interaction is well established. Rats have their territory and usually don't like it when foreign rats try to invade this territory.

How integration proceeds also depends strongly on the characters of the individual rats. Therefore, it is advisable not to change the group, or at least not too much. However, this may be necessary, for example, if one or more rats die and only one or two rats remain from the previous pack.

It is easiest to integrate young animals that no longer need to be with their mother. The ideal age for integrating a new young animal is two to three months. At this age, the rat is old enough to move into a pack and not yet so old that it has already developed distinct territorial behaviour.

In rats, too, the little ones often enjoy "puppy license"; as a rule, young animals are not attacked. In addition, young animals integrate more easily and are more likely to subordinate themselves. Therefore, the risk of a fight is lower than when integrating an adult rat.

© *Sipa*

Purchasing Rats

If you want to get pets, the first way many people go is to a pet shop. This is still very much ingrained in the minds of many people, even though there are much better and more animal-friendly options than the classic pet shop. The more people are educated about the practices of most pet shops, the more they distance themselves from them and are more likely to seek out animal shelters, rescue centres or even reputable breeders.

Pet shops are commercial enterprises that - like any other business - want to make a profit. Therefore, in many pet shops, animals are regarded as commodities and treated as such. Of course, this does not apply to all pet shops and there are also many employees who continue their education and treat the animals well. Nevertheless, making a profit is the top priority.

In very many cases, the animals offered in pet shops come from dubious mass breeding farms where the animals are "produced" under undignified conditions. Nowadays this is quite well documented and there is a wealth of picture material from such breeding farms. As a rule, very little value is placed on species-appropriate husbandry and breeding here. This is not only the case with rats, but also with many other animal species that are offered in the pet trade.

In many cases, the animals have far too little space, are fed unhealthy and cheap food and often develop diseases. Dead animals are often not removed, and the cages are rarely cleaned. Therefore, quite a lot of animals in pet shops show diseases, either due to genetic defects, as serious breeding requires a lot of expertise, or due to the poor keeping conditions in the breeding farms. There are quite a few mass breeding farms where the conditions are very similar to those in factory farming of pigs, for example.

Cannibalism is also not uncommon in such breeding farms, because the animals are often very desperate, hungry, suffer from diseases and have little space.

Now it is only logical and understandable that one feels sorry for these animals. Given the circumstances, many people are not aware that these animals often suffer, or they want to save them. The idea is laudable. However, it must be noted that these practices are supported with every purchase; even if the purchase was made out of compassion and love for animals. We live in capitalism, where demand strongly determines supply. If we now imagine that no one would buy animals from dubious mass breeding farms or from classic pet shops anymore, this business model would no longer be profitable, and breeders and pet shops would be forced to change the way they treat animals. Either the mass animal trade would slowly die out completely or the companies would have to massively improve their practices in order to generate demand again. Therefore, it is in the power of every single animal lover to improve the fate of animals born in the future.

Consequently, the question arises where one can obtain pets in good conscience. The best options are animal shelters on the one hand and rescue centres on the other. Both shelters and rescue centres are full of animals that are no longer wanted by their previous owners, have been abandoned, and so on. Therefore, the most logical and sensible thing to do is to offer these animals a new and nice home first. Reputable breeders are also an option, but many people find it more sensible to give existing animals in animal shelters and rescue centres a new chance first, instead of breeding more and more animals, of which a certain proportion will end up in rescue stations and animal shelters.

In animal shelters and rescue centres, there are mostly somewhat older or adult animals. However, there are also young animals, for example from unintentional mating, which have been abandoned. Some of these animals are quite easy to care for, others are a little more difficult; this is often due to the fact that many animals in shelters and emergency stations have experienced little or no love in the past.

Especially for beginners, rescue centres are in many cases preferable to animal shelters, as rescue centres can often offer better advice and also aftercare than animal shelters. Animal shelters mainly take care of dogs and cats, so knowledge about small animals is sometimes quite limited - although of course this does not apply to all animal shelters either. Rescue centres, on the other hand, are mostly private people who often have years of experience in caring for the species in question. Many rescue centres focus on a specific species (e.g., guinea pigs, rabbits, hamsters or rats) or at least on only a few different species. Therefore, the operators of such rescue centres are usually very good contacts who are happy to provide advice and expertise, which is particularly beneficial for a newcomer.

Reputable breeders are also a suitable alternative; however, they must be strictly distinguished from pure multipliers. Serious breeders know their animals very well, they know the pedigrees, have a sound knowledge of biology and genetics and make no/low profit. This does not apply to multipliers, as they often put animals together without a well-thought-out plan and then sell the babies without paying attention to the future home.

Nevertheless, even with reputable breeders, a surrender fee (protective fee) is normal and necessary. In this way, the breeders minimise the risk of a spontaneous purchase and at the same time cover (at least in part) their costs for food and the like.

© *Sipa*

The Cage

Rats need space! Lack of space can lead to aggression, disease and depression in rats. Fortunately, a lot of attention is now paid to the minimum dimensions of rat accommodation.

The general rule is that rats need at least half a square metre (*5.4 square feet*) of floor space. An enclosure with a length of one metre (*3.2 feet*) and a width of half a metre (*1.6 feet*) would therefore be suitable.

The German TVT (*Tierärztliche Vereinigung für Tierschutz e.V., Veterinary Association for Animal Welfare*) recommends a minimum floor space of 0.4 square metres (*4.3 square feet*), but you should always bear in mind that rats are very curious, enterprising and active. So, more space is always better!

The minimum dimensions are sufficient for a group of three to four animals. Rats should not be kept alone or only in pairs, as in their natural environment they also live in a group and develop group behaviour. The group should consist of rats of the same gender - i.e., several females or several males.

However, so-called harem keeping is also an option. In this case, a neuter is kept with several females. The male must be castrated, otherwise there would regularly be unwanted offspring. In addition, rats do not differentiate between unrelated rats and related rats - a rat would also mate with its sibling.

If several rat groups are kept, for example one group with only male rats and one group with only female rats, the cages of these groups should be far away from each other; at best in different rooms. Otherwise, the two groups might see and especially smell each other, which is often a stress factor.

The height of the rat cage is also important, as rats like to climb and are not strictly ground dwellers. While they are very good at climbing, they are not good at jumping and can easily injure themselves when they fall.

Therefore, a rat cage should have a minimum height of 120 centimetres (*4 feet*); however, a few full tiers are needed to prevent the rats from injuring themselves if they do fall. Full tiers are as large as the footprint of the rat enclosure. Either use only full tiers to minimise the risk of falling and to provide maximum space or combine some full tiers with partial tiers.

The floors should be solid and not made of mesh, as the rats can naturally injure their little feet when walking on lattice bars. It could also cause rats to develop the disease "Bumblefoot". This foot inflammation is very painful for the animals. Furthermore, the floors should be arranged so that the animals cannot fall more than forty centimetres (*1.3 feet*).

However, in some circles a minimum cage height of 100 centimetres (*3.2 feet*) is recommended. This should be the absolute minimum. There are no legal regulations on this yet. Ideally, the rats should be given as much space as possible, so 120 centimetres (*4 feet*) or more is definitely better.

The enclosure needs at least the following equipment:

- Food bowl

- Several hutches

- Drinking bowls or bottles

- Ladders to the higher floors

- Relaxation facilities, such as hammocks or boards for lying on

- Hiding places such as cardboard or wooden tubes

- Bedding (at least in one corner, if not in the whole cage)

- Gnawing material (e.g., twigs)

One might think of providing a running wheel for the active rats - as is compulsory for hamsters. However, rats do not need running wheels. These are usually too small anyway, so that the rat's back is bent in an unnatural way, and this can lead to health problems.

The rat's tails can also get in the way when running in a wheel and pose a risk of possible injury. The spine would be severely damaged by this in the long run.

By the way: The rat's tail also contains bones! It is an extension of the spine, and this runs to the end of the tail. Running balls and jogging balls should also be avoided.

Either the entire enclosure should be lined with litter or at least a small part of it - for example, you can put a litter tray filled with litter in the cage. Both commercial small animal litter and hemp or linseed litter are suitable.

You can also line part of the enclosure with newspaper, for example. Rats also like to use newspaper to line their houses and build nests in it. Unscented cellulose is also suitable for building nests.

Whether the rats should be offered hay and/or straw is quite controversial. Some rats are allergic to it or sneeze a lot because of the dust. Therefore, the bedding should also be dust-free. As a rule, offering hay or straw is not a problem, although hay is usually softer and more comfortable.

The water in the drinking trough should be changed daily and offered fresh. Whether to use water bottles or water bowls is an individual decision. There are rats that prefer to drink from bottles and rats that prefer to drink from a bowl. Of course, both options can be used at the same time.

In any case, the drinking place should be cleaned regularly; especially in drinking bottles bacteria can collect quite quickly and sometimes even algae can form. Ideally, chemical cleaning agents should not be used - vinegar is a good cleaning agent.

Furthermore, make sure that the rat cage is not exposed to draughts. Rats, like other small animals, are quite sensitive and quickly catch colds, which in turn can quickly develop into pneumonia.

In the cage, you should offer so many retreats (little houses, tubes, etc.) that each rat has at least one hiding place. If the group consists of four rats, four hiding places should be provided. More is always better, as this gives the rats more choice.

Many rat keepers also offer their animals a space to run free. This is a very welcome change for the curious rats. This area can be individually designed but should be safe. Rats like to nibble and climb, so it must be ensured that they cannot fall out of windows or nibble on cables.

© Karsten Paulick

Activities

Rats are extremely active and curious animals. In addition, they are also very intelligent. Therefore, they should be encouraged and challenged in their development; boredom can lead to depression and unnatural behaviour in rats. If a rat is too bored, it often develops strange behaviour. For example, it gnaws on the cage bars or runs in circles because it has nothing to do.

For small animals, there are now quite a few activity products on the market. Intelligence toys are especially interesting for rats. However, it is not always necessary to use expensive toys; many activities can also be made from inexpensive materials. Larger activities that do not fit into the cage can be offered outside of the cage.

Let's take a closer look at a few ideas!

1. Labyrinths are very popular. These can also be made from simple cardboard boxes - rats, or animals in general, are not very picky about this. Sometimes simple cardboard toys are even more popular than expensive bought toys. Small pieces of food can be hidden in the maze so that the rats have to search for them. Small treats increase the sense of achievement. However, care should be taken that no toxic glue or needles or similar are used in the construction of the mazes, which could injure the rats.

2. Cardboard boxes can also be turned into burrowing boxes. If you fill them with toilet paper, old newspapers or similar things, rats like to dig around in them. You can also hide treats here so that the rats are busy looking for them.

3. Sandboxes for digging are also quite popular. A box, for example made of hard plastic, can be filled with sand. Cardboard boxes are less suitable for this, as the sand often comes out of the edges and can make a mess. Suitable sand is, for example, commercially available chinchilla sand, fine bird sand or fine building sand.

4. Tubes and tunnels! Rats love to run through tubes and tunnels. The diameter should be at least eight centimetres so that the rats do not get stuck and/or panic. Of course, a larger diameter is also fine. The tunnels should not be too long either, so that the rats do not "pile up" in them and become stressed. It is better to offer several slightly shorter tunnels. These can be made of clay, cardboard or hard plastic - as long as the plastic is not gnawed on by the rats. Old tin cans can theoretically also be used, but they are often sharp-edged, which is dangerous!

5. Fabric toys are also often quite popular with rats and are suitable as long as the rats do not gnaw, destroy or even eat the fabric. For cats, for example, there are so-called "rustle tunnels" on the market that are also well suited as toys for rats. Old trousers can also be used - for example, the legs of old trousers can be converted into a toy. And it is always nice and cosy.

6. As rats are very intelligent, it is easy to teach them little tricks that they will enjoy. The classic trick is "standing on one's hind feet". To do this, hold a treat above the rat's head so that it can only reach you if it stands on its hind legs. If it does not understand this at first, the treat can be held just above its nose and then slowly brought upwards so that the rat follows the treat and therefore stands upright.

7. A similar trick is that the rat must first turn in a circle to receive its treat. This is done by slowly guiding the hand with the treat around the rat so that it has to follow the hand.

8. Especially in summer, rats often enjoy a shallow water bath with treats. To do this, a shallow casserole dish or similar shallow container can be filled with water - only deep enough to allow the feet to cool, but not to get the rat completely wet. In the shallow water bath, you can now let pieces of fruit or vegetables such as cucumber slices float. The rats like to fish these out and it is also refreshing in hot summer months. Please only offer when it is really very warm and the rats need cooling down - if it is too cold, the rats will easily catch a cold.

Of course, there are many more ways to keep rats busy - there are no limits to creativity! The main thing is not to let them get bored for long periods of time, as this can cause the curious and studious rats to become mentally stunted, depressed and suffer health problems due to monotony.

© *Karsten Paulick*

Diet and Nutrition

Rats are omnivorous animals. This means that they are neither pure carnivores nor pure herbivores. Rats eat "everything" and are therefore dependent on both plant and animal food for a healthy and species-appropriate life.

Other popular pets are often pure carnivores or pure herbivores. The cat eats only animal food. Rabbits and guinea pigs eat only plant food. Therefore, in order to feed rats a healthy and balanced diet, attention must be paid to the right proportions and - as always - to the balance of the food.

The healthy diet of rats consists largely of carbohydrates. These provide the rats (and humans) with a lot of energy. Different types of cereals are most important here.

The protein needs of rats should be met by both plant and animal foods. Cooked pulses, for example, have a very high protein content. Animal protein in the form of mealworms can be offered to the rats as a supplement.

The ratio of the individual macronutrients should be approximately as follows:

- About 60% **carbohydrates** (→ plant-based)

- About 20% **protein** (→ mix of plant protein and animal protein)

- About 10% **dietary fibre** (crude fibre) (→ from plants)

- About 5% **fat**

The remaining 5% can be distributed individually.

In addition, care should be taken to ensure a sufficient supply of micronutrients - i.e., vitamins and minerals. To ensure that the rats are supplied with all essential micronutrients, attention must be paid to a varied diet.

Your rats do not need to be fed a new type of food every day, but a variety of choices should be offered - i.e., some different vegetables, different grains, etc.

In addition, rats absorb some vitamins - such as vitamin K and B vitamins - by sometimes eating their own faeces. This is a completely normal and natural behaviour. Animals that engage in this behaviour are called "autocoprophages". This means that they do not eat the faeces of other animal species ("allocoprophages"), but their own faeces. Besides the rat, autocoprophages also include, for example, the guinea pig and the rabbit. This behaviour should not be prevented.

However, one can keep an eye on whether the rats consume an unnatural amount of faeces, because this could indicate a nutrient deficiency, which they try to compensate for by eating a lot of their droppings.

© *Jarle Eknes*

Since carbohydrates make up the main part of the rat diet, most food consists of dry ingredients. The dry food can either be bought "ready-mixed" or composed from the individual ingredients. If you buy ready-mixed food, you should pay close attention to the composition of the individual ingredients, because you will often find unhealthy additives in it. Some examples of unhealthy additives that no rat needs are:

- E150: E-numbers are found on many foods and identify a particular ingredient. E150 - with the additions a to d - simply stands for sugar, as it is also used in cola and sweets. Small amounts of sugar are of course okay, but usually the amount is so high that eating it is very unhealthy for the rats and they quickly become fat. This can lead to other diseases such as heart disease, diabetes, etc.

- Extrudates: Extrudates are very starchy and consist of vegetable by-products. "Vegetable by-products" is a nicer word for "waste". They are produced during the production of other foods and cannot be used any further. However, in order not to have to dispose of them, "vegetable by-products" are usually added to animal feed in order to make some profit from them after all. They are also often found in guinea pig and rabbit feed. Often the pressed, baked vegetable by-products are then coloured to make them look pretty and encourage people to buy them. Because extrudates are so starchy, they fatten up quickly but have no added nutritional value. Extrudates are also very bad for dental abrasion because they do not need to be chewed thoroughly, swell up quickly and make you feel full accordingly. Ergo: The rats eat less raw fibre-rich food, which is so important for the teeth.

- Animal by-products: We have already talked about vegetable by-products, which are simply a waste product. In addition, there are also animal by-products that are produced during the production of meat products and cannot be used any further. These are usually parts of the animal such as feet, tails, eyes and the like. In order to make a profit from these residual products, they are often added to animal feed.

- Molasses: Molasses is sugar syrup, so similar to "E150" it simply stands for sugar.

- Sodium chloride: Sodium chloride is common salt. In the long run, this can cause lasting damage to important organs such as the liver and kidneys.

A healthy dry food should consist of different types of cereals or grains. It often contains dried fruit and vegetables and sometimes animal proteins in the form of dried mealworms and the like. Nuts are also found quite often. Nuts contain healthy fats, but in excess they are also real fatteners - since rats need very little fat anyway, a very small proportion of nuts is sufficient.

Many rat owners mix their own food. The advantage of this is that you know exactly which foods are in there – and you can vary it better. The mixing ratio of a good dry food mix should be approximately as follows:

- about 80% cereals and seeds (popular: wheat, rye, oats, spelt, buckwheat, barley)

- about 10% herbs, flowers, leaves (popular: dandelion, nettle, dill)

- about 8% nuts and seeds (popular: sunflower seeds, pumpkin seeds, hazelnuts)

- about 2% animal proteins (popular: dried mealworms, dried crayfish)

In addition to dry food, rats need daily fresh food in the form of vegetables and fruit. Fruit is naturally sugarier than vegetables, so the majority of the fresh food should be vegetables, supplemented by some fruit now and then.

Which vegetables are good for feeding rats?

- Cucumbers

- Pumpkin

- Corn (fresh)

- Carrots

- Peppers (all colours, without the green stalk
→ stalk is poisonous)

- Tomatoes (without the green stalk → stalk is
poisonous)

- Courgettes

Which types of fruit are suitable, for example?

→ Please all without seeds!

- Apples

- Apricots

- Bananas (very sugary!)

- Pears

- Strawberries

- Mango

- Plums

- Grapes

Highly acidic foods should either not be fed at all or only rarely in small quantities. These include, for example, kiwi, pineapple and berries. Lettuce should also not be offered in abundance. If lettuces are fed, ideally varieties that are quite nutrient-rich should be chosen. These are mainly bitter lettuces. Iceberg lettuce offers little added value and is quite low in nutrients.

From time to time, rats are also allowed to eat a bit of potato, but - as with humans - these should definitely be cooked before eating. The same applies to pasta, although potatoes are healthier than pasta.

Protein intake is already well covered by the plant food and animal proteins in mealworms and the like. However, you can also offer the rats a boiled egg from time to time. This usually goes down well with rats as an occasional treat.

Rats are also usually happy about fresh herbs. Experience has shown that the extremely healthy dandelion is particularly popular. Both the leaves and the flower and stem of the dandelion can be offered.

Sometimes it is criticised that dandelion has too much calcium and that this can promote calcium deposits, which can lead to urinary and kidney stones and bladder sludge. However, this is only true if the rats are fed an unspecific and unhealthy diet.

Normally, if rats are fed a species-appropriate and varied diet, such diseases will not develop, as too much calcium is simply excreted by the rat. This happens through the urine. With a species-appropriate diet, the rat takes in enough water to simply flush out excess calcium.

And what fresh foods should rats not eat?

- Citrus fruits such as lemon etc.

- Avocados

- Spicy vegetables like radishes, radish, onions

Of course, adequate water supply is also part of a species-appropriate diet. The rats should always have the opportunity to drink water. Although they take in water through fresh food, this is often not enough - especially in warmer months.

Whether to use drinking bottles or drinking bowls is an individual decision and quite controversial. Some rats prefer to drink from bowls, some prefer to drink from bottles and some rats don't care. Of course, both options can be offered. The main thing is that the water is always fresh and changed daily. The drinking places also need to be cleaned regularly, because bacteria and sometimes algae collect quite quickly in drinking troughs - primarily in the tube. Chemical cleaning agents should be avoided; vinegar is sufficient and does not pose a health risk.

© Kira Hoffmann

Medical Conditions

Rats - like all animals - can fall ill with many different diseases. They are comparatively sensitive, so the rats should always be closely observed so that the first symptoms of disease can be identified early.

Parasites are quite common in rats. A distinction must be made between endoparasites and ectoparasites.

The reproductive products of the endoparasites are excreted with the rat faeces. They are therefore located inside the rat. Ectoparasites, on the other hand, are found in or on the skin of the animal. They can also "burrow" into the skin. But how does a parasite infestation occur in the first place if rats are kept as pets isolated in the home and have no direct contact with other animals or the environment outside the home?

There is either direct or indirect transmission of the parasites. Infected animals can transmit parasites to the other animals without an intermediate station, for example through physical contact or through the droppings of the diseased rat. On the other hand, parasites can also be introduced into the group via objects or food. You can bring parasites from outside to inside on your shoes, they can be on your hands, they can be transmitted by flies and other insects. The risk can be reduced by good hygiene, but never completely eliminated.

In case of a parasite infestation, it is important to examine and treat all animals in the group. Not all parasite-infested animals show external symptoms. As with humans, the immune system of rats is quite variable, and some animals are more susceptible - especially animals that are more sensitive and easily stressed. It is very likely that the whole group is affected by the parasites, even if not all animals develop symptoms. However, if only the rats with external symptoms are treated, the parasites on/in the healthy rats are not eliminated and could easily be transmitted back.

The treatment of a parasite infestation should therefore be carried out by a competent veterinarian. He will be able to clearly identify the type of parasite and initiate appropriate treatment methods. In the following, we will take a brief look at some of the most common parasites (in alphabetical order).

© *Gordon Johnson*

1. Tapeworms belong to the endoparasites. The tapeworm lives in the digestive tract of the rat and usually causes (sometimes extreme) weight loss and digestive disorders such as constipation or diarrhoea. Tapeworms are usually transmitted to the rat through intermediate hosts, for example, mites or fleas.

2. Fur mites belong to the ectoparasites. In case of infestation, rats usually suffer from itching and sometimes also from dandruff. The itching occurs mainly in the head area and on the back.

3. Hair follicle mites also belong to the ectoparasites. Due to hair follicle mite infestation, the animals often lose hair or fur, and the skin usually turns dark; especially in the head area and on the back. Hair follicle mites are extremely small and therefore cannot be seen without a microscope.

4. Eoccidiosis (endoparasites) usually occurs in young animals that have not yet reached the age of six months. The animals usually suffer from diarrhoea and lose a lot of weight. The diarrhoea causes the body to dry out quite quickly, which in the worst case can lead to the death of the animal. Since these are endoparasites, a faecal examination is mandatory. The expert veterinarian will then treat the infestation with appropriate medication.

5. Like all mites, itch mites belong to the ectoparasites. In case of an infestation with itch mites, the itching from which the animals suffer is extremely severe. The frequent and excessive scratching usually causes severe wounds on the body. Bald patches in the fur are also frequently observed. Itch mites are most often found in other animals, so these parasites are usually transmitted to the rats from other pets.

6. Liver hairworms, like all worms, are endoparasites. In most cases, liver hairworms are transmitted from cats to other animals; usually directly via the cats' faeces. As the name suggests, liver hairworms usually cause severe pain in the area of the rat liver and the tissue of this organ is altered.

7. Ear mites usually cause the so-called "cauliflower ears". These are so called because blisters often form on the ears of rats and crusts and thickenings also occur on the ears. The infestation is therefore quite easy to recognise even for a layperson.

8. Oxyurosis is another type of worm infestation. Diseased animals often suffer from constipation and experience extreme itching around the anal region. This sensitive area is often injured by scratching to relieve the itching.

9. Rat lice are, as the name suggests, a specific rat disease. They belong to the ectoparasites, i.e., they live on/in the skin of the rat. The animals suffer from severe itching, which usually occurs in the head area and extends over the back, and from anaemia. Rat lice can usually be detected with the naked eye. For a layperson, it can be difficult to distinguish between lice and mites; this is another reason why – as always – expert treatment by a veterinarian is necessary.

10. Rat lungworms are also a specific rat disease. These endoparasites first use fish, amphibians or snails as intermediate hosts and then pass on to the rat as the final host. Infestation with rat lungworms affects the respiratory tract and can cause sometimes severe lung problems. Furthermore, inflammation of the body is often caused by the worms.

11. Tropical rat mites belong to the ectoparasites. They cause severe itching and usually also anaemia. They can often be seen with the naked eye; also because they are red or dark when they are full of blood. Unlike some other mite species, tropical rat mites infest the host (i.e. the rat) only at night and hide during the day - similar to bed bugs, for example. Since they do not necessarily need a host to survive, the entire environment must be thoroughly cleaned.

In principle, the parasites presented can also pass on to humans and infest them. This even applies to special rat parasites such as rat lungworms and tropical rat mites. The effect of the infestation also depends on the immune system of the individual. Nevertheless, no risk should be taken. Even if the animals are healthy, you should always wash your hands with soap before touching them. Afterwards, the hands should also be washed.

Parasite infestation is, of course, not the only disease that rats can suffer from. Below we take a closer look at some other common rat diseases.

1. Tumours:

A tumour can occur even in the best cared for and happiest rats; even with the best health and excellent hygiene, it is possible for a rat to develop a tumour. Therefore, prevention is extremely important. You should palpate your rats completely every now and then, looking for hardened areas. If you notice an unusually hard spot under the skin or a small hard bump, you should visit the vet and have it checked out. The tumour may need to be surgically removed.

2. Abscesses:

Abscesses can be mistaken for tumours, especially if the abscess feels hard. Unlike tumours, however, abscesses are collections of pus that are caused by bacteria. Similar to a tumour, an abscess can also occur in any part of the body. In most cases, abscesses are caused by external injuries such as bites or cuts on sharp objects, sharp branches or the like. Bacteria can enter the body through the open wound and possibly cause an infectious abscess. Even if the rat scratches itself frequently and heavily, an abscess can develop through these minor skin injuries. This is another reason why it is important to regularly palpate the rat and look for hard or enlarged areas on the body. Whether it is a tumour or an abscess will be assessed by the vet. Not all abscesses need to be treated surgically, this is always a case-by-case decision. In any case, it is important that the pus is drained properly so that the abscess does not burst and possibly cause blood poisoning.

3. Fungus:

If a rat has a fungus, round hairless patches are often found on the body. The skin is usually scaly or has scabs. Fungus may also be accompanied by hair loss only - or scaly patches of skin may be found on hairless parts of the body such as the ears. Fungal infections can be caused by poor hygiene and lack of air circulation, but many animals also suffer from fungal infections that have psychological causes. This can be due to too much stress, fear or other negative feelings, for example. A poor mental state also weakens the immune system, which can also cause fungal infections. For a layperson, it is usually difficult to distinguish between a fungus, mites or similar. Therefore, a visit to the vet is indispensable. Please also note that a fungus is contagious and can be transmitted to humans as well as to other pets. Therefore, hygiene is also a top priority here.

4. Colds:

Colds must be taken very seriously in rats. The small rat body is not as robust as the human body, for example, so a cold can also very quickly cause dangerous pneumonia, which in the worst case can be fatal. The same applies to other small animals such as hamsters, guinea pigs or rabbits. A cold must therefore be counteracted very quickly, as the aggravation is usually much faster than in humans. The symptoms are the same as in all mammals: Colds show themselves through sneezing, a runny nose, watery eyes, rattling breathing and similar cold symptoms. To prevent colds, draughts should be avoided completely. The rats should also not be exposed to excessive temperature fluctuations. Nevertheless, of course, always make sure that the rat room is well ventilated. Stress or a lack of hygiene can also promote colds.

5. Diarrhoea:

Diarrhoea can have various causes. In rats and similar small animals, diarrhoea does not only occur when the faeces are watery, but also when the shape and/or consistency of the faeces change. Healthy droppings are rounded and elongated. The consistency is firm and almost dry. Fresh droppings are naturally somewhat moist. Diarrhoea also weakens the animal so that the rat may appear tired, not be as active as before or take in less food and water. There may also be cloudy eyes and weight loss.

Diarrhoea is very serious and should be checked by a vet. Particularly if the rat refuses water and food and if the diarrhoea lasts longer than a day, urgent action should be taken.

© *Mustafa Shehadeh*

The most common causes of diarrhoea:

- Too rapid a change of food - Any change of food should be done slowly. Do not offer your rats too much of a new food at the beginning but increase the size of the portions slowly. This is especially true for fresh food that the rats have not yet experienced.

- Mouldy food: For this reason, you should check your supply of dry food regularly to make sure it does not show signs of mould. Mouldy fresh food should also be removed from the cage. Cutting the fresh food into rather small pieces is a good way to prevent mould, as the worst that can happen is that the food dries out.

- Worm infestation or other parasites: Small worms can often be seen on the droppings with the naked eye, but the droppings should always be checked and analysed by a vet if parasite infestation is suspected.

- Poisonous plants or plastic parts: If a rat comes into contact with poisonous plants in the home and gnaws on them, this can lead to symptoms of poisoning, often accompanied by diarrhoea. The same applies to gnawing on plastic parts.

- Stress: If a rat is exposed to stressful situations, it can cause it enormous mental stress. A depressed mental state can spill over into physical health and often causes digestive problems such as diarrhoea.

6. Mycoplasmosis:

Mycoplasmosis is a very common disease in rats; it is the disease that has been documented most frequently in relation to rats. Mycoplasmosis is an infection of the respiratory tract. When a rat is infected, it does not necessarily show symptoms (even at the beginning), so identification is sometimes quite difficult. Furthermore, the disease is very contagious and can easily spread to all animals in the group. The symptoms resemble typical cold symptoms. The rats sneeze often, and the nose runs. If the disease is not treated, there is a great risk that the pathogens will travel further through the respiratory tract to the lungs. This can lead to respiratory distress and even pulmonary embolism. Breathing becomes very difficult and there may be pain when breathing. The rats try not to move too much and to conserve their strength. Mycoplasmosis is comparable to influenza in humans. How well the disease can be fought off also depends very much on how good the animal's (or the human's) immune system is. Prevention is the be-all and end-all here: if you pay attention to a healthy and varied diet, avoid draughts and extreme fluctuations in room temperature, and if the rats are not exposed to too much stress (stress extremely weakens the immune system!), the risk can be reduced quite well.

7. Dental problems:

Rats have a total of 16 teeth, of which the upper and lower incisors grow permanently. The molars do not grow continuously. It is therefore essential that the incisors are always well worn so that they do not grow too long - as this can cause serious health problems. It is also important that the rat's teeth are in the correct position. This means that the teeth automatically rub against each other when feeding. Raw fibre-rich food is therefore very important, because it must be chewed long and thoroughly - this means that the teeth are rubbed down well. However, if a rat has misaligned teeth, the abrasion does not occur evenly and sharp edges can develop on the teeth, which can injure the oral cavity, for example. The rat may suffer from toothache and sometimes even be hindered in feeding by too long incisors. At the latest when the rat no longer eats much - or even at all - it is high time to visit the vet. For prevention, the teeth can be checked by the vet once or twice a year.

© Karsten Paulick

Legal Notice

This book is protected by copyright. Reproduction by third parties is prohibited. Use or distribution by unauthorised third parties in any printed, audio-visual, audio or other media is prohibited. All rights remain solely with the author.

Author: Alina Daria Djavidrad

Contact: Wahlerstraße 1, 40472 Düsseldorf, Germany

© 2021 Alina Daria Djavidrad

1st edition (2021)

© Colleen O'Dell

Room for Notes